Leveled Texts

For Second Grade

Consultants

Kristy Stark, M.A.Ed.
Reading Level Consultant
Long Beach, California

Wendy Conklin, M.A.
Gifted Education Consultant
Round Rock, Texas

Dennis Benjamin
Special Education Consultant
Prince William County Public Schools, Virginia

Marcela von Vacano
English Language Learner Consultant
Arlington County Schools, Virginia

Publishing Credits

Corinne Burton, M.A.Ed., *President*; Conni Medina, M.A.Ed., *Managing Editor*; Emily Rossman Smith, M.A.Ed., *Content Director*; Angela Johnson, M.F.A., M.S.Ed., *Editor*; Robin Erickson, *Multimedia Designer*; Kevin Pham, *Production Artist*; Danielle Deovlet, *Assistant Editor*

Image Credits

pp.17, 19, 21 Creative Commons Martin Luther King's Birthplace by Jim Bowen, used under CC BY 2.0; pp.18, 20, 22 Stan Wayman/The LIFE Picture Collection/Getty Images; pp.42, 44, 46 Diana Rich/Dreamstime; pp.47, 49, 51 Ronnie Kaufman/Larry Hirshowitz; pp.72, 74, 76 PhotoAlto/Alamy; pp.113, 115, 117 (top) Hemant Mehta/age fotostock, (bottom) Everett Collection/Newscom; pp.114, 116, 118 J.R. Bale/Alamy; All other images from iStock, Shutterstock, or the public domain.

Standards

Shell Education
A division of Teacher Created Materials
5301 Oceanus Drive
Huntington Beach, CA 92649–1030
http://www.tcmpub.com/shell-education
ISBN 978–1–4258–1629–2
©2016 Shell Educational Publishing, Inc.

Table of Contents

What Is Differentiation?

Over the past few years, classrooms have evolved into diverse pools of learners. Gifted students, English language learners, special-needs students, high achievers, underachievers, and average students all come together to learn from one teacher. The teacher is expected to meet their diverse needs in one classroom. It brings back memories of the one-room schoolhouse during early American history. Not too long ago, lessons were designed to be one size fits all. It was thought that students in the same grade learned in similar ways. Today, teachers know that viewpoint to be faulty. Students have different learning styles, come from different cultures, experience a variety of emotions, and have varied interests. For each subject, they also differ in academic readiness. At times, the challenges teachers face can be overwhelming, as they struggle to figure out how to create learning environments that address the differences they find in their students.

What is differentiation? Carol Ann Tomlinson (2014, 1) describes the challenge of differentiation as reaching out to "students who span the spectrum of learning readiness, personal interests, and culturally shaped ways of seeing and speaking about and experiencing the world." Differentiation can be carried out by any teacher who keeps the learners at the forefront of his or her instruction. The effective teacher asks, "What am I going to do to shape instruction to meet the needs of all my learners?" One method or methodology will not reach all students.

Differentiation encompasses what is taught, how it is taught, and the products students create to show what they have learned. When differentiating curriculum, teachers become the organizers of learning opportunities within the classroom environment. These categories are often referred to as content, process, and product.

- **Content:** Differentiating the content means to put more depth into the curriculum through organizing the curriculum concepts and structure of knowledge.

- **Process:** Differentiating the process requires the use of varied instructional techniques and materials to enhance the learning of students.

- **Product:** When products are differentiated, cognitive development and the students' abilities to express themselves improve.

Teachers should differentiate content, process, and products according to students' characteristics. These characteristics include students' readiness, learning styles, and interests.

- **Readiness:** If a learning experience aligns closely with students' previous skills and understanding of a topic, they will learn better.

- **Learning styles:** Teachers should create assignments that allow students to complete work according to their personal preferences and styles.

- **Interests:** If a topic sparks excitement in the learners, then students will become involved in learning and better remember what is taught.

How to Differentiate Using This Product

The leveled texts in this series help teachers differentiate language arts, mathematics, science, and social studies content for students. Each section has five passages, and each passage is written at three different reading levels. (See page 8 for more information.) While these texts are written on three reading levels, all levels remain strong in presenting subject-specific content and vocabulary. Teachers can focus on the same content standard or objective for the whole class, but individual students can access the content at their instructional levels rather than at their frustration levels.

Determining your students' instructional reading levels is the first step in the process. It is important to assess their reading abilities often so students are instructed on the correct levels. Below are suggested ways to use this resource, as well as other resources in your building, to determine students' reading levels.

- **Running records:** While your class is doing independent work, pull your below-grade-level students aside, one at a time. Individually, have them read aloud the lowest level of a text from this product (the circle level) as you record any errors they make on your own copy of the text. Assess their accuracy and fluency by marking the words they say incorrectly and listening for fluent reading. Use your judgment to determine whether students seem frustrated as they read. Following the reading, ask comprehension questions to assess their understanding of the material. If students read accurately and fluently and comprehend the material, move them up to the next level and repeat the process. As a general guideline, students reading below 90% accuracy are likely to feel frustrated as they read. There are also a variety of published reading assessment tools that can be used to assess students' reading levels using the oral running record format.

- **Refer to other resources:** You can also use other reading level placement tests, such as the Developmental Reading Assessment or the Qualitative Reading Inventory, to determine your students' reading levels. Then, use the chart on page 8 to determine which text level is the best fit for each student.

Teachers can also use the texts in this series to scaffold the content for their students. At the beginning of the year, students at the lowest reading levels may need focused teacher guidance. As the year progresses, teachers can begin giving students multiple levels of the same text to allow them to work independently to improve their comprehension. This means that each student would have a copy of the text at his or her independent reading level and a copy of the text one level above that. As students read the instructional-level texts, they can use the lower texts to better understand the difficult vocabulary. By scaffolding the content in this way, teachers can support students as they move up through the reading levels. This will encourage students to work with texts that are closer to the grade level at which they will be tested.

General Information About Student Populations

Below-Grade-Level Students

As with all student populations, students who are below grade level span a spectrum of abilities. Some of these students have individualized education plans, while others do not. Some below-grade-level students are English language learners (ELLs), while others are native English speakers. Selected students receive intervention and/or support services, while many other students do not qualify for such services. The shift toward inclusive classrooms has caused an increase in the number of below-grade-level students in the general education classrooms.

These students, regardless of abilities, are often evaluated on the same learning objectives as their on-grade-level peers, and their learning becomes the responsibility of classroom teachers. The following questions come to mind: How do classroom teachers provide this population with "access to texts that allows them to perform like good, proficient readers" (Fountas and Pinnell 2012, 2)? How do classroom teachers differentiate for this population without limiting access to content, grade-level vocabulary, and language? Pages 132–136 give tangible strategies to support this student population.

On-Grade-Level Students

Often, on-grade-level students get overlooked when planning curriculum. More emphasis is placed on students who struggle and, at times, on those students who excel. Teachers spend time teaching basic skills and even go below grade level to ensure that all students are up to speed. While this is a noble thing and is necessary at times, in the midst of it all, the on-grade-level students can get lost in the shuffle. Providing activities that are too challenging can frustrate these students, and on the other hand, assignments that are too easy can seem tedious. The key to reaching this population successfully is to find the right level of activities and questions while keeping a keen eye on their diverse learning styles. Strategies can include designing activities based on the theory of multiple intelligences. Current brain research points to the success of active learning strategies. These strategies provoke strong positive emotions and use movement during the learning process to help these students learn more effectively. On-grade-level students also benefit from direct teaching of higher-level thinking skills. Keep the activities open ended so that these students can surprise you with all they know. The strategies described on pages 137–138 were specifically chosen because they are very effective for meeting the needs of on-grade-level students.

General Information About Student Populations *(cont.)*

Above-Grade-Level Students

All students should be learning, growing, and expanding their knowledge in school. This includes above-grade-level students, too. But they will not grow and learn unless someone challenges them with appropriate curriculum. In her book *Differentiating the Language Arts for High Ability Learners*, Joyce Van Tassel-Baska (2003, 2) stresses that "the level of curriculum for gifted learners must be adapted to their needs for advancement, depth, and complexity." Doing this can be overwhelming at times, even for experienced teachers. However, there are some strategies that teachers can use to challenge the gifted population. These strategies include open-ended questions, student-directed learning, and extension assignments. See pages 139–140 for more information about each of these strategies.

English Language Learners

Acquiring a second language is a lengthy process that integrates listening, speaking, reading, and writing. Students who are newcomers to the English language are not able to deeply process information until they have mastered a certain number of language structures and vocabulary words. Even after mastering these structures, English language learners need to be immersed in rich verbal and textual language daily in school. Students may learn social language in one or two years. However, academic language takes up to eight years for most students to learn. Teaching academic language requires good planning and effective implementation. Pacing, or the rate at which information is presented, is another important component in this process. English language learners need to hear the same words in context several times, and they need to practice structures to internalize the words. Reviewing and summarizing what was taught are absolutely necessary for English language learners' success in the future (August and Shanahan 2006). See pages 141–143 for more information about each of the strategies mentioned here.

How to Use This Product

Readability Chart

Title of the Text	Circle	Square	Triangle
What Are Rainforests?	0.9	2.8	4.8
Dr. Martin Luther King Jr.	1.1	2.9	4.9
Sarah's Journal	0.8	2.6	4.2
Your Guide to Superheroes	0.9	2.4	4.2
The World's Fastest Computer	1.0	2.4	4.5
Lots of Boxes	0.9	2.9	4.7
Planning a Harvest Lunch	0.9	2.5	4.4
Getting Around on the Water	0.7	2.7	4.8
Markets in India	0.8	2.9	4.6
City Gardens	1.0	2.8	4.3
Water!	1.0	2.6	4.1
What Makes a Habitat?	1.0	2.6	4.1
Pollination	0.9	2.5	4.2
Rocks and Minerals	0.8	2.8	4.2
Solids	0.9	2.3	4.2
Rules to Live By	0.7	2.3	4.0
Trade Today	0.8	2.7	4.2
Lead the Way!	0.9	2.5	4.2
Using Maps	0.8	2.6	4.4
Young Abigail Adams	0.9	2.9	4.4

Correlation to Standards

The Every Student Succeeds Act (ESSA) mandates that all states adopt challenging academic standards that help students meet the goal of college and career readiness. While many states already adopted academic standards prior to ESSA, the act continues to hold states accountable for detailed and comprehensive standards.

Shell Education is committed to producing educational materials that are research and standards based. In this effort, all products are correlated to the academic standards of the 50 states, the District of Columbia, and the Department of Defense Dependent Schools. Shell Education uses the Mid-continent Research for Education and Learning (McREL) Compendium to create standards correlations. Each year, McREL analyzes state standards and revises the compendium. By following this procedure, they are able to produce a general compilation of national standards. A correlation report customized for your state can be printed directly from the following website: **www.tcmpub.com/administrators/correlations/**.

8

How to Use This Product *(cont.)*

Components of the Product

The Leveled Texts

- There are 20 topics in this book. Each topic is leveled to three different reading levels. The images and fonts used for each level within a topic are the same.

- Behind each page number, you'll see a shape. These shapes indicate the reading levels of each piece so that you can make sure students are working with the correct texts. The reading levels fall into the ranges indicated below. See the chart on page 8 for the specific level of each text.

Levels
0.7-1.1

Levels
2.3–2.9

Levels
4.0-4.9

Comprehension Questions

- Each level of the texts includes a comprehension question. Like the texts, the comprehension questions were leveled by an expert. They are written to allow all students to be successful within a whole-class discussion. The questions are closely linked so that teachers can ask multiple questions on the topics and all students will be able to participate in the conversations about the texts. The below-grade-level students might focus on the facts, while the above-grade-level students can delve deeper into the meanings of the texts.

How to Use This Product *(cont.)*

Tips for Managing the Product

How to Prepare the Texts

- When you copy these texts, be sure you set your copier to copy photographs. Run a few test pages and adjust the contrast as necessary. If you want the students to be able to appreciate the images, you will need to carefully prepare the texts for them.

- You also have full-color versions of the texts provided in PDF form on the Digital Resource CD. (See page 144 for more information.) Depending on how many copies you need to make, printing full-color versions and/or copying from a full-color version might work best for you.

- Keep in mind that you should copy two-sided to two-sided if you pull the pages out of the book. The shapes behind the page numbers will help you keep the pages organized as you prepare them.

Distributing the Texts

- Some teachers wonder about how to hand out the texts within one classroom. They worry that students will feel insulted if they do not get the same papers as their neighbors. The first step in dealing with these texts is to set up your classroom as a place where all students learn at their individual instructional levels. Making this clear as a fact of life in your classroom is key. Otherwise, the students may constantly ask about why their work is different. You do not need to get into the technicalities of the reading levels. Just state it as a fact that every student will not be working on the same assignment every day. If you do this, then passing out the varied levels is not a problem. Just pass them to the correct students as you circle the room.

- If you would rather not have students openly aware of the differences in the texts, you can try these strategies for passing out the materials.

  - Make a pile in your hands from the circle to triangle level. Put your fingers between the levels. As you approach each student, you pull from the correct section to meet his/her reading level. If you do not hesitate too much in front of each desk, the students will probably not notice.

  - Begin the class period with an opening activity. Put the texts in different places around the room. As students work quietly, circulate and direct students to the correct locations for retrieving the texts you want them to use.

  - Organize the texts in small piles by seating arrangement so that when you arrive at a group of desks you will have just the levels you need.

What Are Rainforests?

Rainforests are like most forests. They have trees. They have plants. But they are wet.

Most rainforests get a lot of rain. They are warm most of the time. Trees and plants grow well. These are tropical (TRAH-pih-kuhl) rainforests.

Other forests are wet, but not from the rain. They get water from fog and the air. These are temperate (TEM-puhr-uht) rainforests. They are not too warm. And they do not get too cold.

Think About It!

What are the names of two different types of rainforests?

What Are Rainforests?

Rainforests are like other forests. They are filled with trees and plants. But they are different in one special way. They are very wet.

Most rainforests get a lot of rain. They are also warm most of the time. This helps trees and plants stay healthy. These are called tropical (TRAH-pih-kuhl) rainforests.

   51629—Leveled Texts for Second Grade

Other rainforests are wet for other reasons. They get water from fog and the moist air near oceans. These are called temperate (TEM-puhr-uht) rainforests. They are not very warm. But they do not get very cold either.

Think About It!
What is the difference between a temperate rainforest and a tropical rainforest?

14

What Are Rainforests?

Rainforests are like other forests because they are filled with trees and plants. But rainforests are different in one special way. They are very wet.

Most rainforests get a lot of rainfall. They are also warm most of the time. In this way, trees and plants stay colorful and healthy. Rainforests like this are called tropical (TRAH-pih-kuhl) rainforests.

Other rainforests are wet, too, but for more reasons than rainfall. They get a lot of water from fog and the moist air that comes from nearby oceans. Rainforests like this are called temperate (TEM-puhr-uht) rainforests. They are not as warm as tropical rainforests, but they do not get very cold either.

Think About It!

How might the differences between the two types of rainforests affect animals?

Dr. Martin Luther King Jr.

Dr. Martin Luther King Jr. was born on January 15, 1929. His home was happy. He felt loved. Martin wrote that his home was a place "where love was central."

But at that time, the world did not show love all the time. African Americans did not have the same rights as other people. People showed hate. They showed fear. This hurt black people.

One time, he was on a full bus. White people got on. He had to give them his seat. He had to stand up for a long time. He was so mad!

The law said that he had to give up his seat. The law was not fair.

Think About It!
What was Martin's home life like?

Dr. Martin Luther King Jr.

Dr. Martin Luther King Jr. was born on January 15, 1929, in Atlanta, Georgia. His home was happy. He and his sister, Christine, and brother, Alfred, felt loved. Martin wrote that his home was a place "where love was central."

But the world was not filled with love all the time. African Americans did not have the same rights as other people. They were hurt because of other people's hatred and fear.

One time, he was riding a full bus. Some white people got on. So Martin had to give up his seat. He had to stand up for 90 minutes. He was so mad!

The law said that he had to give up his seat. But the law was not fair.

Think About It!

How was Martin's home life different from the world around him?

Dr. Martin Luther King Jr.

Dr. Martin Luther King Jr. was born on January 15, 1929, in Atlanta, Georgia. Martin's home was happy. He and his sister, Christine, and his brother, Alfred, felt love all around them. Martin wrote that his home was a place "where love was central."

But the world outside Martin's home was not always filled with love. African Americans were not allowed the same rights as other people. They suffered because of other people's hatred and fear.

Once when Martin was 15, he was riding a full bus. Some white people got on, and Martin had to give them his seat. He rode the bus for 90 minutes standing up. He was very angry!

The law said that Martin had to give up his seat, but the law was unfair and unjust.

Think About It!

What does the author mean by the statement, "But the world outside Martin's home was not always filled with love"?

Sarah's Journal

Saturday, April 15, 1634

Dear Diary,

We are leaving England. We are going to the New World. We are sailing to ~~Massachoo~~ ~~Masachusets~~ Massachusetts (mas-suh-CHOO-suhts) to make a new life. It will take two months to cross the sea if the weather is good. That is eight weeks! We will stay with cousins in Salem. Then, we will buy some land.

The waves are making me ill. Mother is too busy with the little ones to pay heed to me. She wants me to help her. Mary should do that. But she seems sick. Or she wants to avoid her job.

Sarah

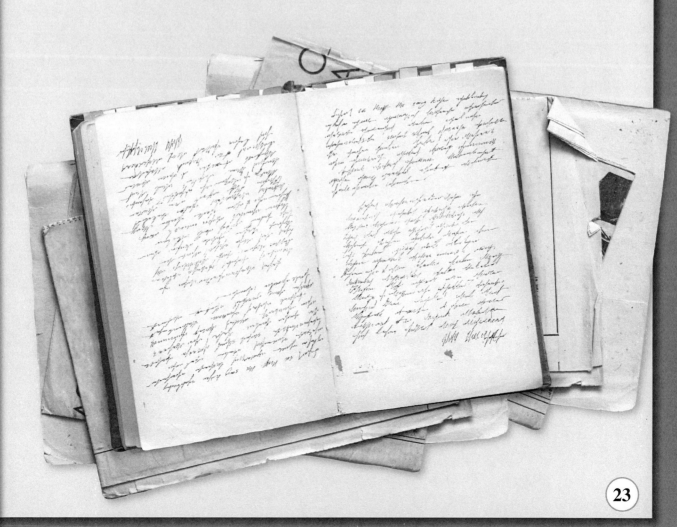

Thursday, June 17, 1634

Dear Diary,

We made it to land. I did not think we would. I thought we were all going to die. Mother and the little ones were sick all the way. I was sick all the way. And so was Mary. Father was not sick. I think his joy kept him well.

I am so glad to be off the ship. It was close to nine weeks at sea. Our cousins met our ship. We made our way by horse and wagon to Salem. The trip was close to 15 miles.

Sarah

Think About It!
How do Sarah and her family feel about crossing the ocean?

(24)

Sarah's Journal

Saturday, April 15, 1634

Dear Diary,

We're sailing to the New World. We are leaving England forever and sailing to ~~Massachoo~~ ~~Masachusets~~ Massachusetts (mas-suh-CHOO-suhts) to make a new life for ourselves. It will take close to two months to cross the Atlantic if the weather is fair. That's eight weeks! We're going to stay with Mother's cousins in Salem. Then, we will buy some land for ourselves.

The motion of the waves is making me feel ill. Mother is too busy with the younger children to pay heed to me. She wants me to help her. Mary should do that, but she seems to be unwell. I think she is making it up to avoid her jobs.

Sarah

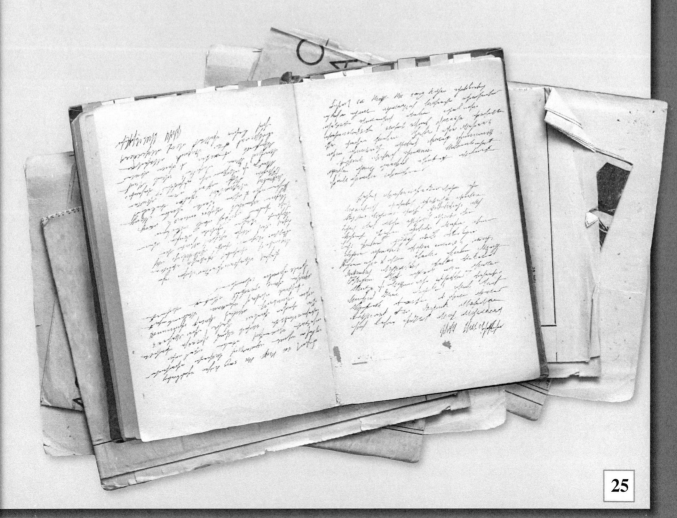

Thursday, June 17, 1634

Dear Diary,

We finally reached land. I never thought we would. I thought I was going to die. I thought we were all going to die. Mother, the little ones, and I were sick all the way. And so was Mary. Father was not sick. I think his joy in going to the New World overcomes all else.

I am so glad to be off the ship, after nearly nine weeks at sea. Our cousins met our ship. We made our way by horse and wagon to Salem, where they live. The journey was almost 15 miles.

Sarah

Think About It!

Why is Sarah so glad to arrive in the New World?

26

Sarah's Journal

Saturday, April 15, 1634

Dear Diary,

We're sailing to the New World. We are leaving England forever and sailing to ~~Massachoo~~ ~~Masachusets~~ Massachusetts (mas-suh-CHOO-suhts) to make a new life for ourselves. It will take nearly two months to cross the Atlantic if the weather is fair and cooperates. That's eight weeks! We're going to stay with Mother's cousins in Salem until we can purchase some land for ourselves.

The motion of the waves is making me feel ill. Mother is too busy with the younger children to pay attention to me. She wants me to help her. Mary should do that, but she seems to be unwell. I think she's pretending to avoid fulfilling her duties.

Sarah

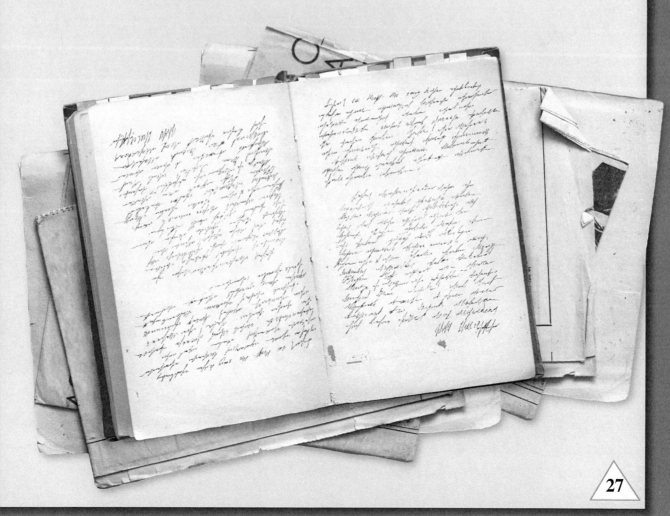

Thursday, June 17, 1634

Dear Diary,

We finally reached land. I never thought we would. I thought I was going to die, and I thought everyone else was going to die. Mother, the little ones, and I were sick the entire way. And so was Mary. Father was not sick. I think his joy and excitement about going to the New World overcome everything else.

I am so glad to be off the ship, after nearly nine weeks at sea. Our relatives met our ship. We made our way by horse and wagon to Salem, where they live. The journey was almost 15 miles.

Sarah

Think About It!
Why do you think Sarah's family is going to the New World?

28

Your Guide to Superheroes

Need to lift books? Are you tired?

Need help with school?

Or a kid who bugs you?

Hire a superhero!

Our team is the best!

There's no problem these heroes cannot fix.

So take a look at their tricks and make your pick.

Call 888-555-HERO to book yours today!

Super Shoulders

Never be weighed down by your backpack again. Strong shoulders means Dr. Bear can carry lots of stuff. Trains? Planes? Cars? You name it! She will even lift pets that are too tired to walk.

Claim to Fame

Dr. Bear once carried a pet rhino home from school. The rhino was tired after Show and Tell. Of course, we all have our limits. Dr. Bear would like to forget that she dropped it in the pool!

Large Lungs

Mr. Puff has huge lungs. He can swim underwater for hours! He can get things from the bottom of the pool. He even saved the rhino once!

Claim to Fame

Mr. Puff likes to play the trombone for hours. It helps him relax. He is best known for playing nine trombones at the same time! *Parp! Parp! Parp!*

Think About It!
What superheroes can you hire?

Your Guide to Superheroes

Are you tired of carrying heavy books?

Do you need help with homework?

Or pesky younger brothers?

Hire a superhero!

From head to toe, our team is the best!

There's no problem these heroes can't fix.

So take a look at all their tricks and make your pick.

Call 888-555-HERO to book yours today!

Super Shoulders

Never be weighed down by your backpack again. Strong shoulders means Dr. Bear can carry just about anything. Trains? Planes? Cars? You name it! She will even carry pets that are too tired to walk.

Claim to Fame

Dr. Bear once carried a pet rhino home from school. The rhino was exhausted after Show and Tell. Of course, everyone has his or her limits. Dr. Bear would rather forget dropping the rhino in the pool!

Large Lungs

Mr. Puff is famous for his huge lungs. He can swim underwater for hours! He is an expert at fetching things from the bottom of the pool. He even saved the rhino!

Claim to Fame

Mr. Puff likes to relax by playing the trombone for hours. He is best known for playing nine trombones at the same time! *Parp! Parp! Parp!*

Think About It!
Why would someone hire Mr. Puff?

32

Your Guide to Superheroes

Are you tired of carrying heavy books?

Do you need assistance with homework?

Or annoying younger brothers?

Hire a superhero!

From head to toe, our team is the best!

There's no problem these remarkable heroes can't fix.

So take a look at all their specialized tricks and make your pick.

Call 888-555-HERO to book yours today!

Super Shoulders

Never be weighed down by your overstuffed backpack again. Powerful shoulders means Dr. Bear can carry just about anything. Trains? Planes? Cars? You name it! She will even carry pets that are too exhausted to walk.

Claim to Fame

Dr. Bear once carried a pet rhinoceros home from school. The rhino was exhausted after Show and Tell. Of course, everyone has his or her limitations. Dr. Bear would rather forget accidentally dropping the rhino in the swimming pool!

Large Lungs

Mr. Puff is famous for his gigantic lungs. He can swim underwater for hours! He is an expert at fetching anything from the bottom of the pool. He even rescued the rhino!

Claim to Fame

Mr. Puff enjoys playing the trombone for hours to relax. He is best known for playing nine trombones at the same time! *Parp! Parp! Parp!*

Think About It!
How are Mr. Puff and Dr. Bear alike? How are they different?

The World's Fastest Computer

There is an amazing computer. It is faster than all other computers. It knows words that you speak. It can read words that you write. And it can come up with new ideas by itself.

This computer can make plans. It can do a lot of things at once. It can even control a whole system. And, it will never shut down. In fact, it works better when it is used more. What is this?

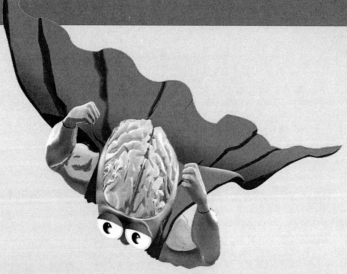

It is your brain, of course! Most animals have brains. But your brain is the most amazing of all brains. It is larger than most animal brains. Your brain is always on the job. Touch your finger to your nose. Clap your hands. Sing a song. You can do all of these things because your brain tells your body what to do. It is like a boss. All the parts of your body are the workers. All you have to do is think a thought. Your brain makes the workers get right to it.

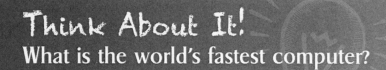

Think About It!
What is the world's fastest computer?

(36)

The World's Fastest Computer

There is an amazing computer. It is faster than any other computer in the world. It can understand speech and writing. It can come up with new ideas.

It makes plans. It can control a whole, complicated system. It can do many things at once. But it will never shut down. In fact, the more it is used, the better it gets. What is this amazing computer?

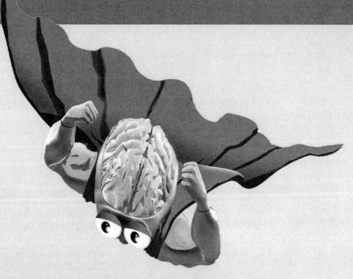

It is your brain, of course! Most animals have brains. But the human brain is the most amazing brain of all. It is larger and more complicated than other animal brains. Your brain is always on the job. Touch your finger to your nose. Clap your hands. Sing a song. You can do all of these things because your brain tells your body what to do. It is like a boss, and all the parts of your body are the workers. All you have to do is think a thought, and your brain makes the workers get right to it.

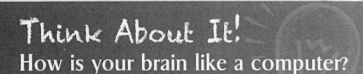

Think About It!
How is your brain like a computer?

The World's Fastest Computer

There is an amazing computer. It is faster than any other computer in the entire world. It can understand speech and writing. It can come up with innovative ideas.

It can make and execute plans. It can control a whole, complicated system and do many things at once without shutting down. In fact, the more it is used, the better it gets. What is this amazing computer?

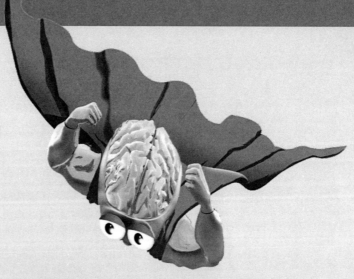

It is your brain, of course! Most animals have brains, but your brain—the human brain—is the most amazing brain of them all. It is larger and more complicated than most other animals' brains. Your brain is always on the job, even when you are asleep. Want to touch your finger to your nose or quickly clap your hands? Are you in the mood to sing a song or dance to the music on your favorite radio station? You can do all of these things, and a great deal more, because your brain instructs your body to do so. Your brain is like a manager, and all the parts of your body are the workers. All you have to do is think a thought, and your brain makes the workers get right to it.

Think About It!

Compare and contrast your brain to an actual computer.

Lots of Boxes

There are eight families who live on Grant Street. One day, things change. There is a moving van with cones near it.

The Drakes move in. All the kids watch. They want to see what is on the truck.

The kids see a lot of big boxes.

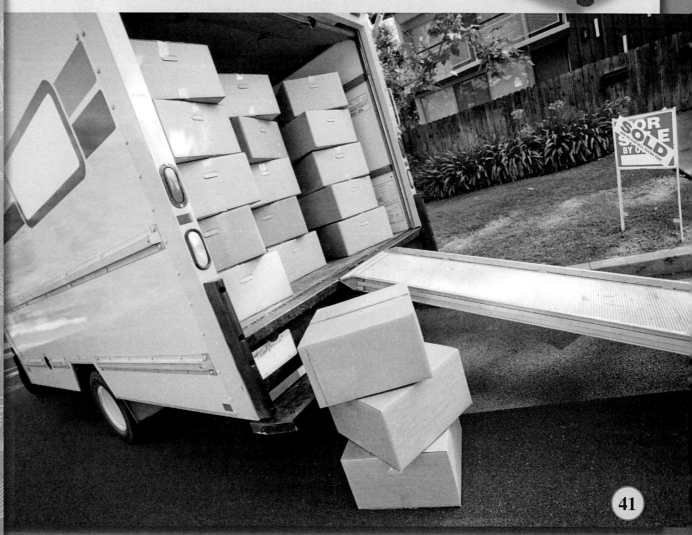

Moving Math

It helps movers to know how big a box is. You can measure the length, the height, and the width. Each of those is a dimension (duh-MEN-shuhn).

Boxes are three-dimensional shapes. They are also called 3-D. Some are cubes. All the edges have the same lengths. Some are rectangular prisms. Those edges are not the same lengths.

Think About It!
How do you measure a box?

Lots of Boxes

There are eight families who live on Grant Street. One day, things change. There is a moving van with cones around it.

The Drakes are moving in. All the kids watch to see what will come off the truck.

The kids see a lot of big boxes.

Moving Math

It sometimes helps movers to know how big a box is. You can measure the length, the height, and the width. Each of those measurements is called a dimension (duh-MEN-shuhn).

Boxes have three dimensions. They are called three-dimensional shapes. Another name for three-dimensional is 3-D. Some boxes are cubes. All the edges are equal lengths. Some boxes are rectangular prisms. The edges on those boxes have lengths that are not the same.

Think About It!

Why is measurement important to a mover's job?

Lots of Boxes

There are eight families who live on Grant Street. One day, things change a lot. The families see a moving van with several traffic cones surrounding it.

The Drake family is moving into the neighborhood. All the other kids watch to see what will come off the truck.

The neighborhood kids see many enormous boxes.

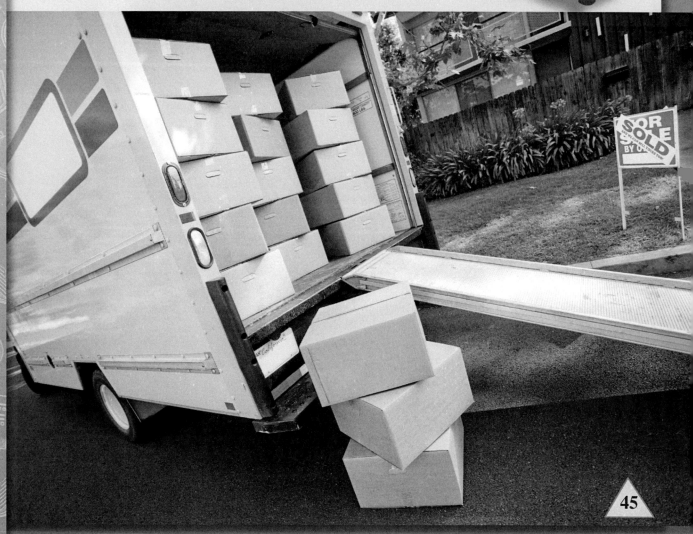

Moving Math

It sometimes helps movers to know how big a box is. You can measure the length, the height, and the width. Each of those measurements is called a dimension (duh-MEN-shuhn).

Boxes have three dimensions. They are called three-dimensional shapes. Another name for three-dimensional is 3-D. Some boxes are cubes. All the edges are equal lengths. Some boxes are rectangular prisms. The edges on those boxes have lengths that are different.

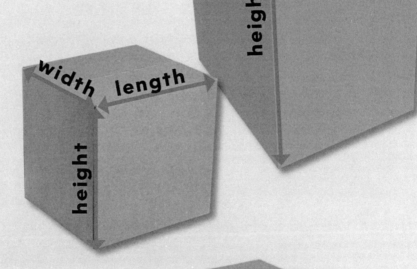

Think About It!
What might happen if a mover does not know how to measure boxes?

Planning a Harvest Lunch

The Garcia kids love autumn. They go to their grandparents' home for a visit. There are lots of huge apple trees at the home. All the kids and adults help pick apples. They make a lot of food with the apples. They end the visit with a harvest lunch.

There are five kids in the family. This year, each kid will invite a friend to come to the lunch. It will be a big lunch!

First, they start to plan. They want to be sure that they have lots of food.

Preparing is busy work. The kids pick apples. They love to climb the ladders.

Harvest Lunch Guest List

Adults	Kids	Kids' Guests
Grandma Garcia	Hector	Adrian
Grandpa Garcia	Diego	Lee
Grandma Kane	Eva	Amy
Mr. Garcia	Rosa	Tess
Mrs. Garcia	Maria	Ana
Lee's mother		
Ana's father		

Then, they plan the menu. They want to have lots of food. They plan some games, too.

Think About It!
What are the kids planning?

48

Planning a Harvest Lunch

The Garcia kids love autumn. They always go to their grandparents' home for a visit. Their grandparents have a huge apple orchard. All the kids and adults help pick apples. They make many different foods with the apples. They end the visit with a harvest lunch.

There are five kids in the Garcia family. This year, each kid gets to invite a friend to come to the lunch. It will be a big lunch!

They start planning early in the week. They want to be sure they prepare enough food.

Monday is very busy. The kids pick apples all morning. They love climbing the ladders best.

Harvest Lunch Guest List

Adults	Kids	Kids' Guests
Grandma Garcia	Hector	Adrian
Grandpa Garcia	Diego	Lee
Grandma Kane	Eva	Amy
Mr. Garcia	Rosa	Tess
Mrs. Garcia	Maria	Ana
Lee's mother		
Ana's father		

During their break after lunch, they plan the menu. They want to make sure there is enough food. They plan some games, too.

Think About It!
Describe the steps the kids take to plan the harvest lunch.

Planning a Harvest Lunch

The Garcia kids love autumn. Every autumn, the Garcia kids go to their grandparents' home for a visit. Their grandparents have a huge apple orchard, and all the kids and adults participate in picking apples. They make many different foods with the crisp, juicy apples. They end their visit with a delicious harvest lunch.

There are five kids in the Garcia family. This year, each kid gets to invite a friend to come to the lunch. It will be a big lunch!

Early in the week, they begin planning the harvest lunch. They want to be sure that they prepare enough food for everyone.

Monday is very busy. The children pick apples throughout the morning. Their favorite part is climbing the ladders.

Harvest Lunch Guest List

Adults	Kids	Kids' Guests
Grandma Garcia	Hector	Adrian
Grandpa Garcia	Diego	Lee
Grandma Kane	Eva	Amy
Mr. Garcia	Rosa	Tess
Mrs. Garcia	Maria	Ana
Lee's mother		
Ana's father		

During their break after lunch, they plan the menu. They want to make sure there is enough food. They plan some fun and interesting games, too.

Think About It!

What are the kids responsible for doing to prepare for the harvest lunch?

Getting Around on the Water

Thousands of years ago, you could have sailed on a Chinese junk. These ships are strong. They are made out of wood. You could still sail on one today!

The hydrofoil below is a fast ship. It goes so fast that it lifts up out of the water.

Chinese junk

hydrofoil

A freighter (FREY-tuhr) is a large ship. It moves goods from place to place. Some have cranes to lift off the goods. Freighters are slow. They take many days to move the goods. This chart shows a trip that a freighter ship may take.

Los Angeles to Spain	Number of Days to Each Port
From Los Angeles to Tokyo	14
From Tokyo to Korea	2
From Korea through the Suez Canal	21
From the Suez Canal to Spain	10

freighter

Think About It!
What are some ways people can get around on water?

Getting Around on the Water

Thousands of years ago, you could have sailed on a Chinese junk. These strong wooden ships still sail on the seas today.

A much faster modern ship is the hydrofoil below. It goes so fast that it lifts up out of the water.

Chinese junk

hydrofoil

55

A freighter (FREY-tuhr) is a large ship. It moves goods around the world. Some large freighters even have cranes to lift off the cargo. Freighters travel slowly. They take many days to deliver goods. This chart shows a trip that a freighter ship may take.

Los Angeles to Spain	Number of Days to Each Port
From Los Angeles to Tokyo	14
From Tokyo to Korea	2
From Korea through the Suez Canal	21
From the Suez Canal to Spain	10

freighter

Think About It!
Which of the water vessels would you take if you needed to get someplace quickly? why?

Getting Around on the Water

Thousands of years ago, you could have sailed on a Chinese junk. These strong, wooden ships still sail on the seas today.

A much faster modern ship is the hydrofoil below. It moves so rapidly that it rises up out of the water.

Chinese junk

hydrofoil

A freighter (FREY-tuhr) is a large cargo ship. A freighter transports goods around the world. Some large freighters even have gigantic cranes to unload the cargo. Freighters travel very slowly. Freighters take many days or several weeks to deliver goods. This chart shows a typical journey that freighters take.

Los Angeles to Spain	Number of Days to Each Port
From Los Angeles to Tokyo	14
From Tokyo to Korea	2
From Korea through the Suez Canal	21
From the Suez Canal to Spain	10

freighter

Think About It!
How are the three water vessels different?

Markets in India

Outdoor markets can be found in India. Items are laid out on mats or in carts. They are set up in bins or bags. Fruits and vegetables are sold there, too.

You can buy cloth. Most of the cloth is light. It is hot there. Cloth is sold by length. In India, length is measured in meters.

59

Spices are sold, too. You do not need to use a lot of spice in foods. So they are sold in small counts by weight. In India, weight is measured in grams.

Think About It!
What types of things are sold at Indian Markets?

Markets in India

Outdoor markets can be found all over India. Items are laid out on blankets or in carts. They are set up in baskets or bags, too. Fruits and vegetables are also sold at markets in India.

Lots of people buy fabric at the markets. Most of the fabric is light. This is because it is hot in India. Fabric is sold by length. In India, length is measured in meters.

61

Markets sell spices, too. You do not need to use a lot of spice in foods. So they are sold in small amounts by weight. In India, weight is measured in grams.

Think About It!

What items might be sold in meters? What items might be sold in grams?

Markets in India

Outdoor markets can be found all over India. Some items are laid out on blankets or in carts. Other merchants set up in baskets or bags. Fruits and vegetables are also sold at outdoor markets in India.

Many people buy colorful fabric at the outdoor markets. Most of the fabric is very light because it is hot in India. Fabric is sold by length. In India, length is measured in meters.

Many markets also sell spices. You do not need to use a lot of spice in foods, so spices are sold in small amounts by weight. In India, weight is measured in grams.

Think About It!

Explain why things are sold by different measurements.

City Gardens

Some people live in cities. They may not have room for gardens. They might live in apartments. Or they could live in a house with a small yard.

If you live in a city and like to eat fresh fruits and veggies, what would you do? You can grow these things!

Some people grow things without yards. They may plant some things in pots. They could also be put on porches or decks. Some people put them in patterns.

Look at the picture below. What pattern do you see?

Some people live on the top floors of buildings. They may make gardens on the roofs. What luck!

Lots of plants can grow on roofs. You can plant a tree or bush in a large pot. Or you can plant vegetables or flowers in small pots.

LET'S EXPLORE MATH

A rooftop garden has bushes and trees. They are put in a pattern against the edge of the roof. The pattern looks like this:

a. What type of plant would come next?

b. What type of plant would be 9th?

Think About It!
What is a city garden?

City Gardens

Many people live in cities. They might not have room for gardens. They may live in apartment buildings or in houses with small yards.

Not having a yard does not stop some people from growing things. They could plant a few things in pots. Plants can be put on a balcony or deck. Some people may put them in patterns.

Look at the picture below. What pattern do you see?

Some people live on the top floors of their buildings. They may make gardens on their roofs. Those people are lucky!

Many different types of plants can grow on rooftops. Trees and bushes can be planted in large pots. Vegetables and flowers can be planted in small pots or flower boxes.

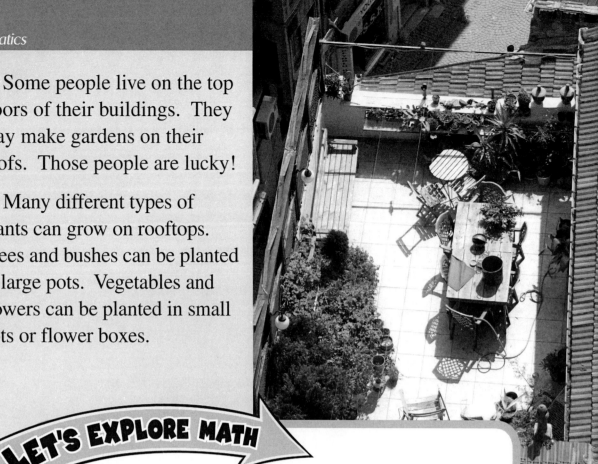

LET'S EXPLORE MATH

A rooftop garden has bushes and trees. They are put in a pattern against the edge of the roof. The pattern looks like this:

a. What type of plant would come next?

b. What type of plant would be 9th?

Think About It!

How can people in a city grow garden fruits and vegetables without having yards?

City Gardens

Many people live in cities. These people may not have enough room for gardens. Some people live in apartment buildings or in houses with very small yards.

However, they still might want to grow fresh fruits and vegetables. What could they do?

Not having yards does not stop some people from growing fruits and vegetables. Plants can be placed in flower pots. They can be put outside on a balcony or deck. Some people may place the pots in patterns. Look at the picture below. What pattern do you see?

Some people live on the top floors of their buildings, so they are able to create gardens on their rooftops. Those people are really lucky!

A wide variety of plants can grow on rooftops. Trees and bushes can be planted in large pots. Vegetables and flowers can be planted in smaller terracotta pots or wooden flower boxes.

LET'S EXPLORE MATH

A rooftop garden has bushes and trees. They are put in a pattern against the edge of the roof. The pattern looks like this:

a. What type of plant would come next?

b. What type of plant would be 9th?

Think About It!

What are some advantages and disadvantages of growing fruits and vegetables in a city?

Water!

All living things need water. Plants need it to grow. Water goes up their roots. Thin tubes carry it up the stems. Water then passes through their leaves. It turns to vapor.

Animals need water, too! They must drink water to live.

water vapor

Water passes through the leaves and turns to vapor.

Water passes through the roots to the leaves.

Humans need water to live. When you drink water, it moves through your body. It keeps you *hydrated*. It keeps you healthy. Some of it leaves your body. This happens when you sweat. This happens when you go to the bathroom, too.

We use water for lots of things. It is not just to drink. It cleans things, like our bodies. We use it to grow food. We need it to cook food. Water can also make power. This is called hydroelectric power. We can use this power to light our homes.

Think About It!
Name three different ways water is used.

Water!

All living things need water. Plants need water to grow, and they get water through their roots. Thin tubes carry the water up their stems. Water then passes through their leaves, and it turns into vapor.

Animals need water, too! They must drink water to live.

water vapor

Water passes through the leaves and turns to vapor.

Water passes through the roots to the leaves.

Humans also need water to live. When you drink water, it moves through your body. It keeps you hydrated. It keeps you healthy. Some of the water leaves your body. This happens when you sweat and when you go to the bathroom.

We utilize water in many ways. It is not just for drinking. We use water to clean things, including ourselves. We need water to grow the food we eat. We use water to cook food. Water can also make power. This is called hydroelectric power. This power can light our homes.

Think About It!
Name three different ways water is used.

Water!

All living things need water. Plants need water to grow, and they get water through their roots. Thin tubes carry the water up their stems. Water then passes through their delicate leaves, and it turns to vapor.

Animals need water, too! They must drink plenty of water to stay alive and be healthy.

water vapor

Water passes through the leaves and turns to vapor.

Water passes through the roots to the leaves.

Human beings also need water to live. When you drink water, it moves throughout your body. It keeps you hydrated and healthy. Some of the water leaves your body when you sweat and when you go to the bathroom.

We use water in many interesting ways. It is not just for drinking. We use water to clean things, including our clothing and our bodies. We use water to grow delicious food, and we use water to cook food. Water can also be used to make electricity. This is called hydroelectric power. We can use that power to light our homes, schools, and businesses.

Think About It!
Name three different ways water is used.

What Makes a Habitat?

The right habitat for a living thing has just what it needs to live well. This means the right soil. It means the right water. It means the right food and light. It means the right climate, too. And it means the right predators!

Things that live on land need the right kind of soil. Plants need soil to grow. Animals need plants for food. Or they eat animals that eat the plants! Animals also need the right kind of land for their shelter.

Plants need water. Animals need water, too. They may need freshwater. They may need saltwater. Plants and animals must live in places that have lots of the water they need.

Living things need the right kind of food. Plants need nutrients from the soil. Plants need light from the sun. Light helps them grow. Animals need to eat to live. Some animals eat plants. Others eat meat. Some eat both. They all need lots of food to live.

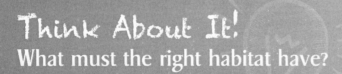

Think About It!
What must the right habitat have?

What Makes a Habitat?

The right habitat for a living thing has exactly what it needs to live well and thrive. This means the right soil, water, food, and light. It means the right climate, too. And it means the right predators!

Things that live on land need the right kind of soil. Plants need soil to grow. Animals need plants for food. Some animals eat animals that eat the plants! Animals also need the right kind of land for their shelter.

 51629—Leveled Texts for Second Grade

Plants and animals need water, too. They may need freshwater. They may need saltwater. Plants and animals must live in habitats that have the right kind of water and plenty of it.

Living things also need the right kind of food. Plants need nutrients from the soil. Plants also need energy from the sun. Light helps them grow. Animals need to eat to live. Some animals eat plants, while others eat meat. Some animals eat both. They all need plenty of food throughout the year to live.

Think About It!
Why do living things need the right habitats?

What Makes a Habitat?

The perfect habitat for any living thing has exactly what it needs to live well and thrive. This means the proper soil, water, food, and light. It means the right climate and temperature. It also means the right predators.

Things that live on land need the right kind of soil. Plants need soil to grow, and animals need plants for food. Some animals eat other animals that eat the plants! Animals also need the right kind of land for their shelters.

Plants and animals need water, too. Some may need freshwater, while others may need saltwater. Plants and animals must live in habitats that have the proper kind of water and plenty of it.

Living things also need the right kinds of food. Plants need nutrients from the soil, and plants need energy from sunlight. Sunlight helps the plants grow lush and healthy. Animals can't absorb food like plants; they need to eat to live. Some animals eat plants, while others eat meat. Some animals eat both plants and other animals. All animals need plenty of food throughout the year to live.

Think About It!
What would happen to the habitats of humans and animals if there were no more plants?

Pollination

Bugs help plants. Wind and water help plants, too. They move pollen from plant to plant. This is called pollination. This helps to make new plants.

Pollen is a dust. It is found at the ends of stamens (STAY-muhns). Stamens are long and thin. They make the pollen. Each stamen has an anther. It holds the pollen.

To make a new plant, pollen must reach the pistil (PIS-tuhl). The *pistil* is the female part of the plant. The stigma (STIG-muh) is at the top of the pistil. The tube below it is the style. The ovary is at the base of the pistil. This is where seeds are made. Petals keep the pistil safe.

The stigma is sticky. Pollen sticks to it. Then, it goes down the style. It goes to the ovary.

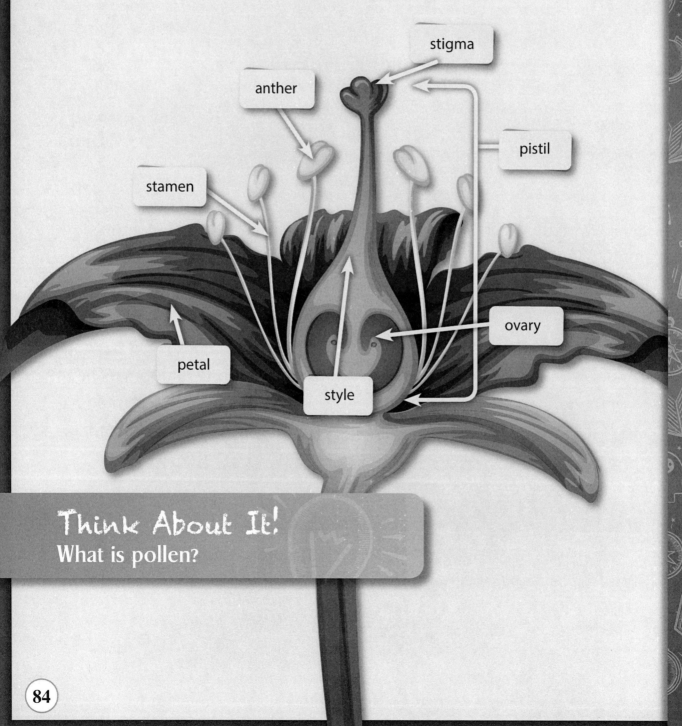

Think About It!
What is pollen?

Pollination

Insects, wind, and water help plants. They do this through pollination. Pollination is how these things carry pollen from plant to plant. Pollination starts the process that allows new plants to grow.

Pollen is a dust. It is found at the end of a flower's stamens. Stamens (STAY-muhns) are long and thin. They make the pollen. On the end of each stamen is an anther. The anther holds the pollen.

To make a new plant, the pollen must reach the pistil (PIS-tuhl). The pistil is the female part of the plant. The stigma (STIG-muh) is at the top of the pistil. The tube below it is the style. The ovary is at the base of the pistil. This is where seeds are made. In many flowers, petals protect the pistil. They surround it. They keep it safe.

The stigma is sticky. Pollen can easily stick to it. Then, it goes down the style. It reaches the ovary.

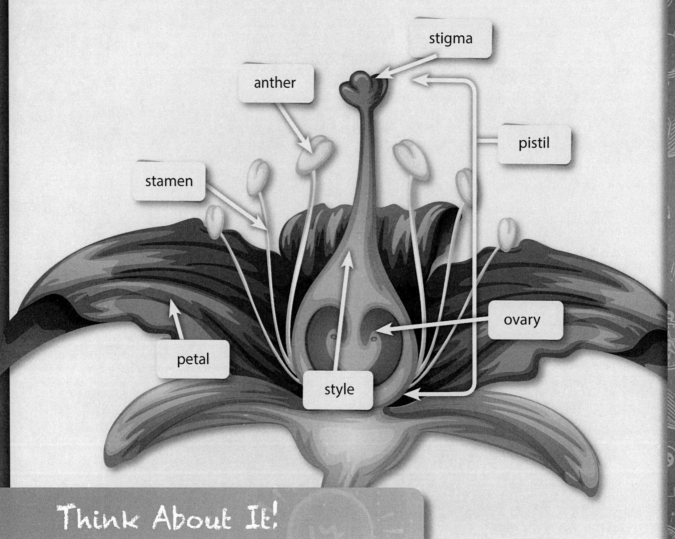

Think About It!
How do insects help spread pollen?

Pollination

Insects, wind, and water help plants. They do this through pollination. Pollination is how these things carry pollen from plant to plant. Pollination starts the process that allows plants to produce additional plants.

Pollen is similar to dust, and it is found at the end of flowers' stamens (STAY-muhns). Stamens are long and thin. They produce the pollen. On the end of each stamen is an anther. The anther holds the pollen.

87

To make a new plant, the pollen must reach the pistil (PIS-tuhl). The pistil is the female part of the plant. The *stigma* (STIG-muh) is at the top of the pistil. The tube below it is called the *style*. The ovary is at the bottom of the pistil. The ovary is where the plant's seeds are produced. In many flowers, petals protect the pistil by surrounding it and keeping it safe.

The stigma is extremely sticky. Because of this stickiness, pollen can easily adhere to it. Then, it goes down the style. It reaches the ovary.

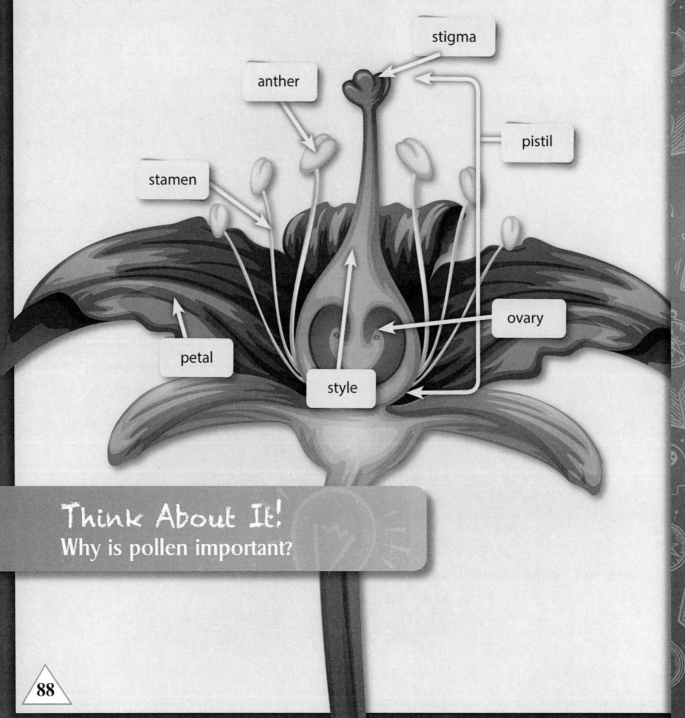

stigma

anther

pistil

stamen

ovary

petal

style

Think About It!
Why is pollen important?

Rocks and Minerals

Look up. Look down. Look all around! Almost anywhere you look, there are rocks. Earth is made of rock. There are rocks in space. Mountains and beaches are made of rocks. Buildings and roads can be made of rocks, too.

Some rocks are young. And some rocks are old. Some rocks are big. Some rocks are small. Some rocks are tough and strong. Other rocks are soft and weak. Rocks can be rough or smooth. Rocks come in lots of shapes and colors. But all rocks have stories to tell.

Have you ever baked a cake? To bake a cake, you need ingredients. You get flour, sugar, and eggs. Then, you mix them all together. The ingredients that make rocks are called *minerals*. Almost all rocks are made of minerals. Minerals are formed underground. Most rocks are made of two or more minerals.

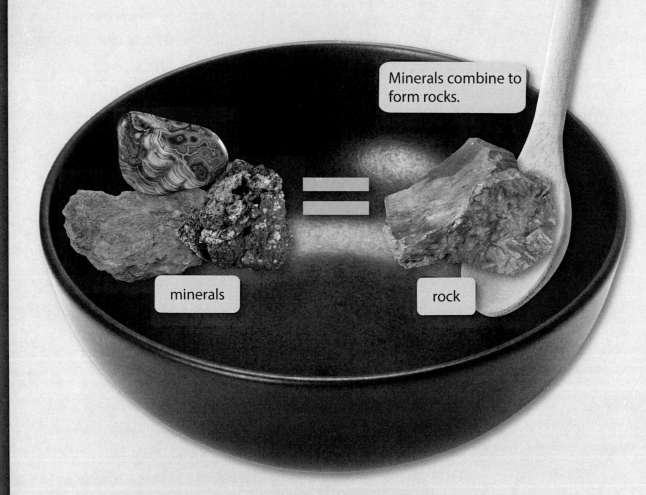

Minerals combine to form rocks.

minerals

rock

Think About It!
What things are made of rocks?

Rocks and Minerals

Look up, down, and all around! Almost anywhere you look, there are rocks. Earth itself is made of rock. There are even rocks in outer space. Mountains and beaches are made of rocks. Buildings and roads can be made of rocks, too.

There are rocks that are young and rocks that are ancient. Some rocks are enormous, and some rocks are tiny. Certain rocks are tough and strong, while others are soft and delicate. Rocks can be really rough or really smooth. Rocks come in various shapes and colors. But all rocks have interesting stories to tell.

Have you ever baked a cake? To bake a cake, you need ingredients. You use things such as flour, sugar, and eggs. Then, you mix them all together. The ingredients that make rocks are called *minerals*. Almost all rocks are made of minerals. Minerals are substances that are formed underground. Most rocks are made of two or more minerals.

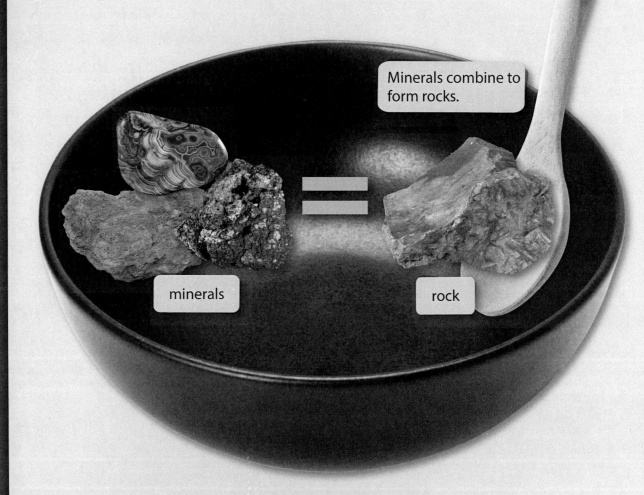

Minerals combine to form rocks.

minerals

rock

Think About It!
How are things made of rocks alike?

Rocks and Minerals

Look up, down, and all around! Almost anywhere you look, there are rocks. Our planet Earth is made of rock. There are even rocks in outer space. Mountains and beaches are made of rocks. Buildings and roads can be made of rocks, too.

There are rocks that are very young, and there are rocks that are ancient. Some rocks are enormous, and some rocks are extremely tiny. Certain rocks are sturdy and strong, while others are soft and delicate. The surface of rocks can be especially rough or really smooth. Rocks can be found in various shapes and colors. But all rocks have interesting stories to tell.

Have you ever helped bake a cake? To bake a cake, you need many ingredients. You use particular ingredients such as flour, sugar, and eggs. Then, you combine and mix the ingredients together. The particular ingredients that make rocks are called *minerals*. Almost all rocks are made of minerals. Minerals are substances that are formed underground over a period of time. Most rocks are made of two or more minerals.

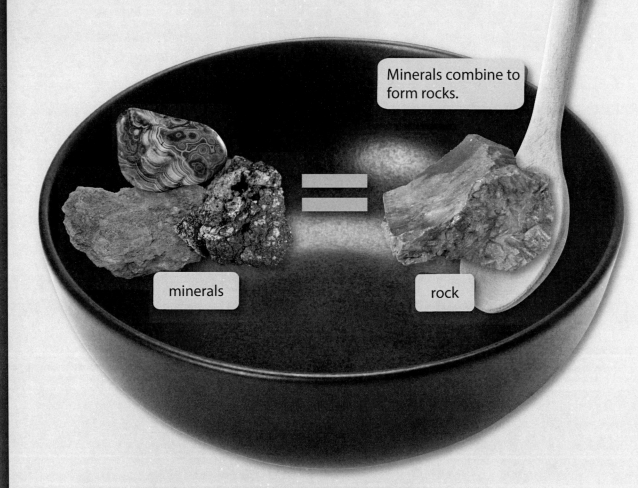

Minerals combine to form rocks.

minerals

rock

Think About It!

Why does the author compare rocks to baking a cake?

94

Solids

A solid can be hard. Or it can be soft. It can be big or small. Salt is a tiny solid. Sand and powder are tiny, too. Walls and roads are solids that are not so small. They are huge.

A solid has its own shape. It will not change to fit to the shape of a jar. So if you fill a jar with beads, each bead will keep its own shape.

You can cut a solid to change its size and shape. You can bend or twist some solids. For example, a rope is a solid. You can make it curved or straight. Clay can be made into a shape. Then, it keeps that shape until you change it.

Solids can be joined to form a new solid. This happens when you use blocks to make a tower. Solids can be taken apart, too. This happens when you knock down the tower.

Think About It!
What are some examples of solids?

Solids

A solid can be hard or soft. It can be big or small. Some solids are tiny. Salt, sand, and powder are tiny solids. Walls and roads are solids that are not so tiny. They are huge!

A solid has its own shape. If you put it into a container, it will not conform to the shape of the container. So if you fill a jar with plastic beads, each bead keeps its own shape.

Cutting a solid changes its size and shape. Some solids can be bent or twisted. For example, a rope is a solid. You can make it curved or straight. Clay can be made into a shape. Then, it keeps that shape until you change it again.

Solids can be joined to form a new solid. This happens when you put building blocks together to make a tower. Solids can be taken apart, too. This happens when you knock down the tower.

Think About It!
What are some characteristics of solids?

Solids

A solid can be hard or soft, and a solid can be big or small. Some solids are tiny. Salt, sand, and powder are examples of tiny solids. Walls and roadways are solids that are not so tiny. Walls and roadways are massive solids.

A solid has its own shape. If you put a solid into a container, it will not conform to the shape of the container. For example, if you fill a bucket with plastic beads, each bead retains its own shape.

Cutting a solid changes its size and shape. Some solids can be bent or twisted. For example, a rope is a solid. You can make it curved or straight. Clay can be made into nearly any shape, and it will keep that shape until you decide to change it into a different shape.

Solids can be joined together to form a new solid. This happens when you put building blocks together to make a tower. Solids also can be taken apart. This happens when you knock down the tower.

Think About It!
Describe how a solid can be changed.

Rules to Live By

Every place has rules. Families have rules at home. Kids may have to clean their rooms. Kids may have to take out the trash. They need to listen to their parents. They have to use good manners.

Schools have rules, too. Students need to show their teachers respect. They can do this by raising their hands before speaking. They need to listen, too. They need to be kind to each other. Rules help keep things running well.

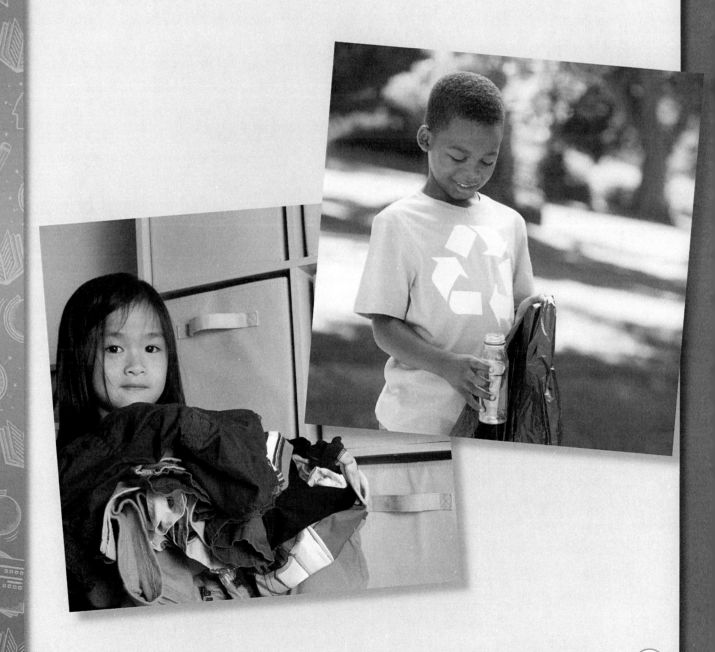

Laws are like rules. People must follow laws. Laws make sure we are safe.

Transportation laws help keep us safe. Cars have to stop at stop signs. Cars have to stop at red lights. We have to cross the street in crosswalks. These laws keep us safe.

Think About It!
What places have rules?

102

Rules to Live By

Every place has rules. Families have rules at home. Kids may have to clean their rooms or take out the trash. They need to listen to their parents. They have to use good manners.

Schools have rules, too. Students need to show their teachers respect. They can do this by raising their hands before speaking. Students need to be good listeners, too. They also need to be kind to their classmates. Following the rules helps keep things running smoothly.

Laws and rules are very similar. People must follow laws. Laws make sure we are safe.

There are transportation laws, too. The transportation laws help keep us safe. Cars have to stop at stop signs and red lights. People have to cross the street in crosswalks. Following these laws keeps people safe.

Think About It!
Why do some places have rules?

Rules to Live By

Every place has rules. Families have rules to follow at home. Kids may have to clean their rooms, take out the trash, or do other chores. They need to listen to their parents, and they have to use good manners.

Schools have rules, too. Students need to be respectful toward their teachers. Students can show respect by raising their hands before speaking and by being attentive listeners. They also need to be kind and courteous to their classmates. Following the rules helps keep things running smoothly.

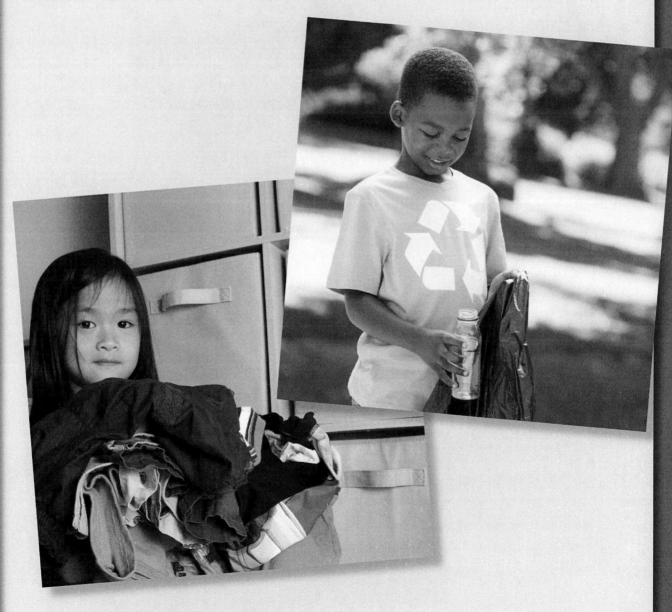

Laws are like rules, which must be followed. Laws protect citizens and help them stay safe.

There are transportation laws, too. For example, cars have to stop at stop signs and red lights, and people have to cross the street in crosswalks. Following these laws keeps people safe.

Think About It!
How do rules keep us safe?

106

Trade Today

Long ago, trade was slow. It took a long time for goods to move from place to place. Trade is much faster now.

Today, ships move cases filled with goods. They can cross the sea in a week. A plane can make the trip in a few hours. Trucks drive goods from town to town. Things move fast!

Today, we are linked to people all around the world. One place can produce goods that other places need. The United States makes things like food and planes. We sell them to other countries.

Other places make goods that we need. They make things like oil and coffee. Countries help each other get what they need.

Think About It!
What things carry goods?

Trade Today

Long ago, trade was slow. It took a long time for goods to move from one place to another. Trade happens much faster now.

Today, ships carry containers filled with goods. They can cross the sea in a week. An airplane can make the trip in just a few hours. Trucks drive goods quickly from town to town in minutes. Things move fast!

Today, we are linked to people all around the world. One country can produce, or make, goods that other countries need. The United States produces things such as food and airplanes. We sell these things to other countries.

Other countries produce goods that the United States needs. They produce things like oil and coffee. Countries depend on each other to get what they need.

Think About It!

Why are goods carried faster today than long ago?

Trade Today

Long ago, trade was extremely slow. It took a very long time for goods to move from one place to another. Nowadays, trade happens much faster.

Today, ships carry gigantic containers filled with many goods. They can cross an entire ocean in a week. An airplane can make the trip in just a few hours. Trucks drive goods from town to town in minutes. Things move quickly!

111

Today, we are linked to people all around the world. One country can produce, or make, goods that are necessities to other countries. The United States produces many things, including food and airplanes. We sell these items to other countries.

Other countries produce goods that the United States needs. They produce things like oil and coffee. Countries depend on each other to get what they need.

Think About It!

Describe how ships and airplanes have linked people around the world.

Lead the Way!

Have you ever played Follow-the-Leader? It is fun. One person is the leader. That person is in charge. He or she leads the way. What can this game teach us about the world we live in?

Traits of a Good Leader

Good leaders are fair. They treat all people with the same respect. Good leaders are caring. They help others. They make good choices. They do the right things. Good leaders are responsible (ree-SPON-suh-buhl). They can choose between right and wrong.

Leaders help keep the peace. They make rules to keep us safe. They make sure we know the rules. Leaders work hard to make the world a good place.

Leaders care about others. They help people in need. They care about the world, too. They try to keep their communities (kuh-MYOO-nih-teez) clean.

Kid Leaders

Kids can lead too! They can help kids in need. They can share food with kids who do not have any. They can pick up trash to keep the city clean. They can lead when they care for others.

Think About It!
What is a leader?

51629—Leveled Texts for Second Grade

Lead the Way!

Have you ever played Follow-the-Leader? It is a fun game. One person is the leader. That person is in charge. He or she leads the way for others to follow. What can this game teach us about the world we live in?

Traits of a Good Leader

Good leaders are fair. They treat all people with the same respect. Good leaders are also caring, and they help others. Good leaders make good choices. They do the right things. Good leaders are responsible (ree-SPON-suh-buhl). They can choose between right and wrong behaviors.

Leaders help people get along with one another. They also make rules to keep people safe. They make sure people follow the rules. Leaders work hard to make the world a better place.

Leaders care about people. They help people in need. They care about the world, too. They try to keep their communities (kuh-MYOO-nih-teez) clean.

Kid Leaders

Kids can lead, too! They can help other kids in need. They can share food with kids who are hungry. They can also pick up trash to keep their communities clean. Kids can be leaders by caring for others.

Think About It!
What makes a good leader?

Lead the Way!

Have you ever played the game Follow-the-Leader? It is a really fun game. One person is the leader, and that person is in charge. He or she leads the way for other people to follow. What can this game teach us about the world we live in?

Traits of a Good Leader

Good leaders are fair. They treat all people in the same respectful manner. Good leaders are also caring, and they help other people. In addition, good leaders make good choices and do the right things. Good leaders are responsible (ree-SPON-suh-buhl). When faced with a choice between right and wrong behaviors, good leaders choose wisely.

Leaders can also help people get along with one another. Leaders also make rules to ensure the safety of other people, and they make sure people abide by, or follow, the rules. Leaders work hard to make the world a better place.

Leaders care about people, and they help people in need. Leaders care about the world, too. They try to keep their communities (kuh-MYOO-nih-teez) clean.

Kid Leaders

Kids can become leaders, too! They can help other kids in need. For example, they can share food with kids who are hungry. They can also collect trash to keep their communities clean. Kids can be leaders by caring for others.

Think About It!
Explain why good leaders are important to the world and to communities.

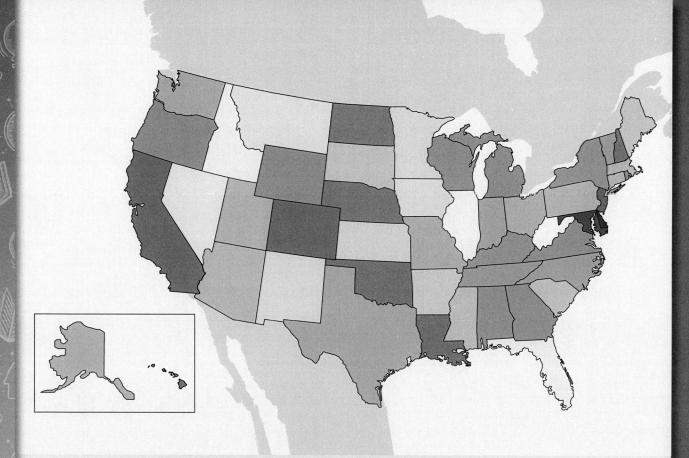

Using Maps

The United States is huge! It goes from the Pacific Ocean to the Atlantic Ocean. It has 50 states. Some states are very large!

We can use maps to learn about the world. Maps help us see the shape of the land. Maps show us a place. Let's look at a map!

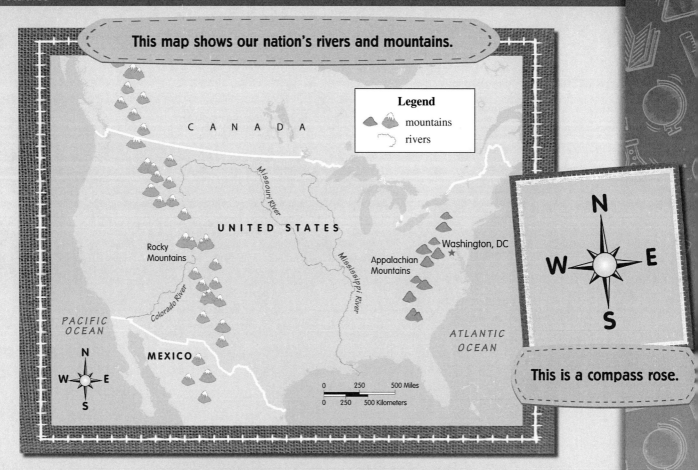

This map shows our nation's rivers and mountains.

This is a compass rose.

There are tools to help us read maps. The legend (LEH-juhnd), or key, shows the marks on a map. It shows the lines and colors, too. A compass rose shows north, east, south, and west.

The scale is a tool, too. It helps us measure distances on a map. If you use these tools, you can read any map!

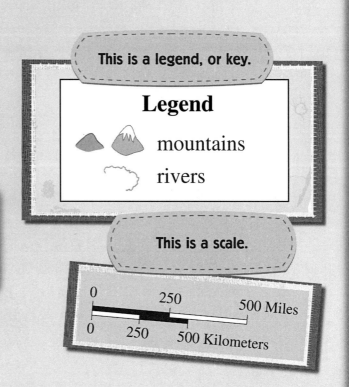

This is a legend, or key.

Legend

mountains

rivers

This is a scale.

Think About It!
What tools help us read maps?

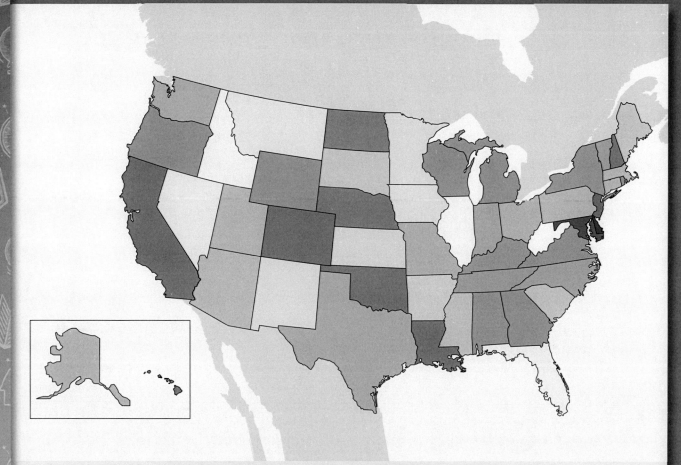

Using Maps

The United States is huge! It stretches from the Pacific Ocean to the Atlantic Ocean. It is made up of 50 states. Some of the states are larger than whole countries!

We can use maps to learn about the world. Maps help us see the shape of the land. Maps also show us important places. Let's explore America!

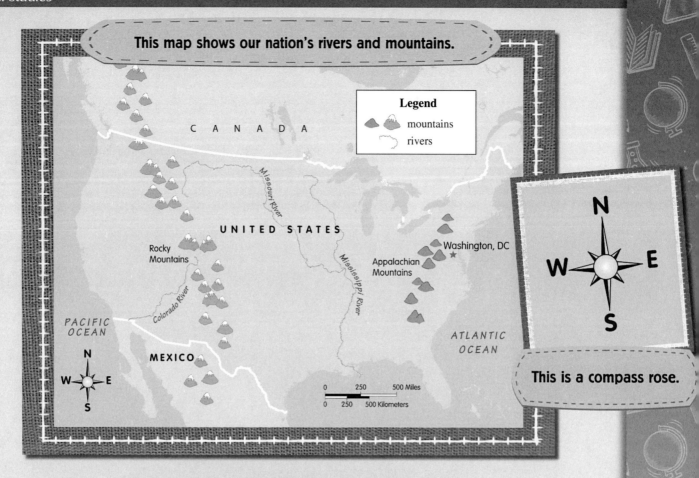

This map shows our nation's rivers and mountains.

Legend
mountains
rivers

CANADA

UNITED STATES

Missouri River

Rocky Mountains

Mississippi River

Colorado River

Washington, DC

Appalachian Mountains

PACIFIC OCEAN

ATLANTIC OCEAN

MEXICO

N W E S

0   250   500 Miles
0   250   500 Kilometers

N W E S

This is a compass rose.

There are tools to help us read maps. The legend (LEH-juhnd), or key, explains the symbols, lines, and colors on a map. A compass rose shows the four directions: north, east, south, and west.

Another tool is the scale. It helps us measure distances on a map. If you know how to use these tools, you can read any map!

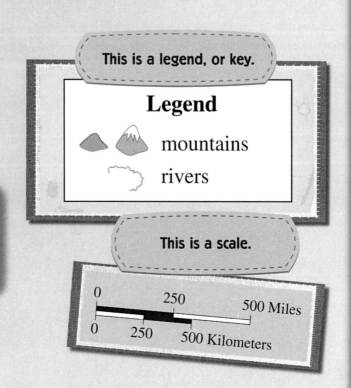

This is a legend, or key.

Legend

mountains

rivers

This is a scale.

0   250   500 Miles
0   250   500 Kilometers

Think About It!
Why are map tools important?

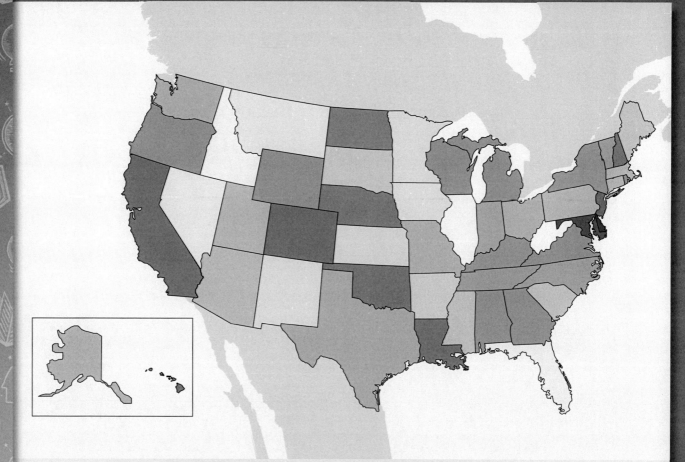

Using Maps

The United States is enormous! It stretches from the Pacific Ocean to the Atlantic Ocean. It is made up of 50 states. Some of the states are larger than entire countries!

We can use maps to learn about countries around the world. Maps help us clearly see the shape of the land, and maps show us important places. Let's explore the United States of America!

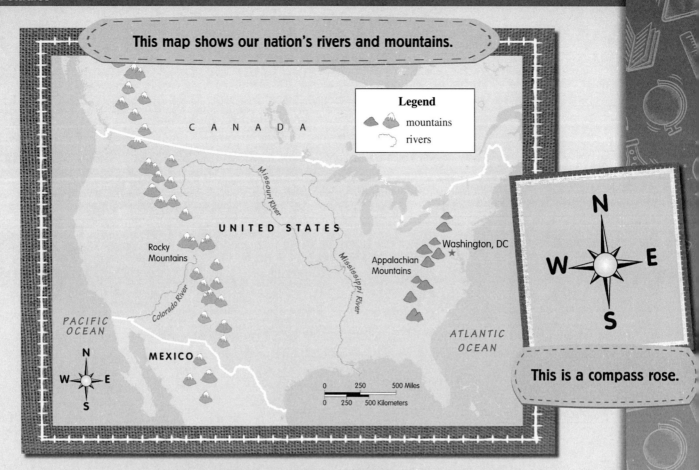

This map shows our nation's rivers and mountains.

This is a compass rose.

There are various tools to help us read maps. The legend (LEH-juhnd), or key, explains the symbols, lines, and colors on a map. A compass rose shows the four directions: north, east, south, and west.

The scale is another important tool. It helps us accurately measure distances on a map. If you know how to use these essential tools, you can read any map!

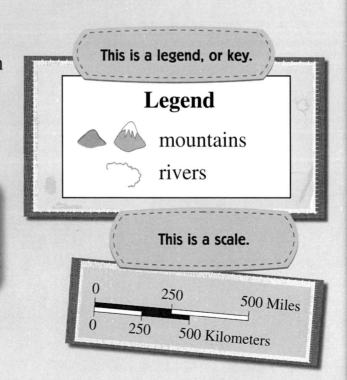

This is a legend, or key.

Legend

mountains

rivers

This is a scale.

Think About It!
Describe how and why we use maps.

Young Abigail Adams

Abigail was brave. She spoke her mind.
She was born on November 11, 1744.
This was in Weymouth (WEY-mehth),
Massachusetts (mas-suh-CHOO-suhts).
She was one of five children.

Her mother cared a lot. She helped others in need. Her father helped others, too. He led a church. Back then, most girls could not go to school. Her mom taught girls in her home. Abigail loved to learn. She read lots of her dad's books.

Think About It!
Where did Abigail learn?

Young Abigail Adams

Abigail Adams was a brave woman. She was not afraid to speak her mind. She was born on November 11, 1744, in Weymouth (WEY-mehth), Massachusetts (mas-suh-CHOO-suhts). She was the second of five kids.

Abigail's mother was caring. She helped families in need. Her dad was a pastor. He was in charge of a church. Back then, most schools did not let in girls. So her mom taught Abigail and her sisters at home. Abigail loved to learn. She read lots of her dad's books.

Think About It!
Why didn't Abigail go to school?

Young Abigail Adams

Abigail Adams was a brave woman who was not afraid to speak her mind. She was born on November 11, 1744, in Weymouth (WEY-mehth), Massachusetts (mas-suh-CHOO-suhts). She was the second of five kids.

Her mother was caring. She helped needy families. Abigail's father was a pastor. He was in charge of a church. Back then, many schools only allowed boys to attend. So Abigail's mother taught her and her sisters at home. Abigail loved to learn and read. She read many of her father's books.

Think About It!

How was life for girls in the 1700s different from today?

References Cited

August, Diane, and Timothy Shanahan. 2006. *Developing Literacy in Second-Language Learners: Report of the National Literacy Panel on Language-Minority Children and Youth.* Mahwah, New Jersey: Lawrence Erlbaum Associates, Inc.

Fountas, Irene, and Gay Su Pinnell. 2012. *The Critical Role of Text Complexity in Teaching Children to Read.* Portsmouth, Virginia: Heinemann.

Tomlinson, Carol Ann. 2014. *The Differentiated Classroom. Responding to the Needs of All Learners, 2nd Edition.* Reston, Virginia: Association for Supervision and Curriculum Development.

Van Tassel-Baska, Joyce. 2003. "Differentiating the Language Arts for High Ability Learners, K–8. ERIC Digest." Arlington, Virginia: ERIC Clearinghouse on Disabilities and Gifted Education.

Vygotsky, Lev Semenovich. 1978. "Interaction Between Learning and Development." In *Mind in Society*, 79–91. Cambridge, Massachusetts: Harvard University Press.

Strategies for Using the Leveled Texts

Throughout this section are differentiation strategies that can be used with each leveled text to support reading comprehension for the students in your classroom.

Below-Grade-Level Students

KWL Charts

KWL charts empower students to take ownership of their learning. This strategy can be used as a pre- or post-reading organizer and a tool for further exploration or research on a topic. Guide students with the following questions:

- What can scanning the text tell you about the text?
- What do you know about the topic of this text?
- What do you want to know about this text?
- What did you learn about the topic?
- What do you still want to know about the topic? (*extension question*)

what do you KNOW?	what do you WANT to know?	what did you LEARN?

Strategies for Using the Leveled Texts *(cont.)*

Below-Grade-Level Students *(cont.)*

Vocabulary Scavenger Hunt

Another prereading strategy is a Vocabulary Scavenger Hunt. Students preview the text and highlight unknown words. Students then write the words on specially divided pages. The pages are divided into quarters with the following headings: *Definition*, *Sentence*, *Examples*, and *Nonexamples*. A section called *Picture* is put over the middle of the chart. As an alternative, teachers can give students selected words from the text and have them fill in the chart individually. (Sample words can be found on page 134).

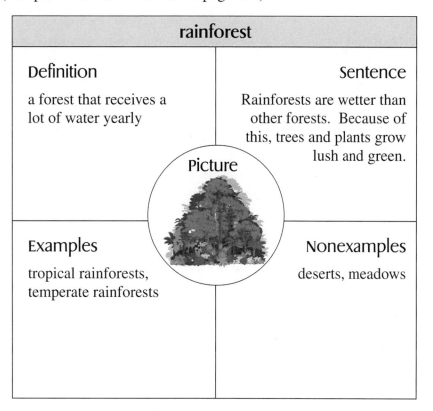

This encounter with new vocabulary words enables students to use the words properly. The definition identifies the word's meaning in student-friendly language, which can be constructed by the teacher and/or student. The sentence should be written so that the word is used in context. This sentence can be either one students make up or copied from the text in which the word is found. This helps students make connections with background knowledge. Illustrating the word gives a visual clue. Examples help students prepare for factual questions from the teacher or on standardized assessments. Nonexamples help students prepare for *not* and *except for* test questions such as "All of these are examples of rainforests *except for* . . ." and "Which of these examples is *not* a rainforest?" Any information students are not able to record before reading can be added after reading the text.

Strategies for Using the Leleveled Texts *(cont.)*

Below-Grade-Level Students *(cont.)*

Frontloading Vocabulary and Content

As an alternative to the Vocabulary Scavenger Hunt, teachers can frontload, or pre-teach, vocabulary or content in a text prior to reading. This can be a useful tool for all students, especially below-grade-level students who struggle with on-demand reading and comprehension tasks. Activate students' prior knowledge by asking:

- What do you know about the word/topic …

- All these words are about the text you are going to read. Based on these words, what do you think the text will be about?

The words below can be used during frontloading discussions before reading a text. (Note: Some words are not found in all levels but can be used to focus students' attention toward the theme and main idea of text they will read.)

Text	Words, Themes, and Content
What Are Rainforests?	forests, rainforests, tropical rainforests, temperate rainforests
Dr. Martin Luther King Jr.	hate, love, unjust, prejudice
Sarah's Journal	ill, New World, immigration
Your Guide to Superheroes	superhero, assistance, limitations
The World's Fastest Computer	system, complicated, execute, plans
Lots of Boxes	dimensions, 3-D, prisms
Planning a Harvest Lunch	harvest, prepare, responsible, autumn
Getting Around on the Water	freighter, transportation, hydrofoil, junk
Markets in India	markets, grams, meters
City Gardens	garden, produce, variety
Wonderful Water	vapor, electricity, hydrated
What Makes a Habitat?	predators, prey, nutrients
Pollination	pollination, stigma, stamens, pistil
Rocks and Minerals	minerals, ancient, delicate
Solids	solid, conform, massive
Rules to Live By	rules, courteous, attentive, respect
Trade Today	trade, necessities, transport, produce, goods
Lead the Way!	leader, responsible, communities
Using Maps	tools, distances, compass
Young Abigail Adams	First Lady, women's rights, activist

Strategies for Using the Leveled Texts (cont.)

Below-Grade-Level Students (cont.)

Graphic Organizers to Find Similarities and Differences

Setting a purpose for reading content focuses the learner. One purpose for reading can be to identify similarities and differences. This skill must be directly taught, modeled, and applied. Many of the comprehension questions in this book ask students to compare and contrast. The chart below can be used to respond to these questions.

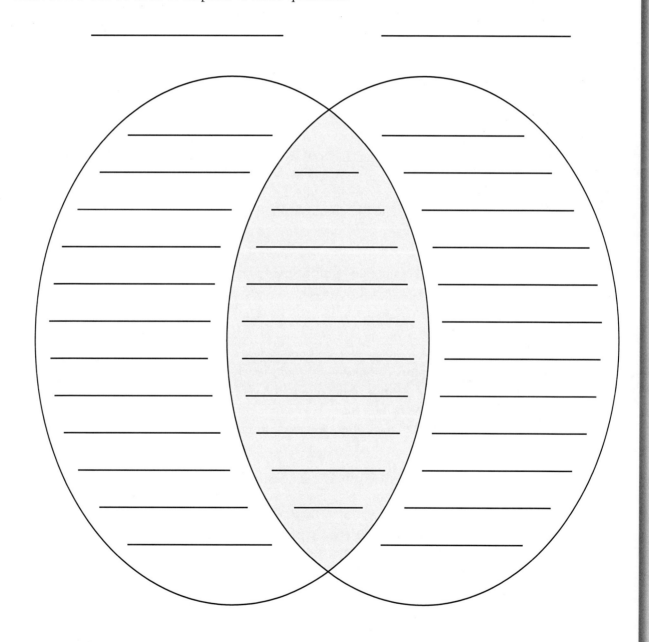

135

Strategies for Using the Leveled Texts *(cont.)*

Below-Grade-Level Students *(cont.)*

Framed Outline

This is an underused technique that yields great results. Many below-grade-level students struggle with reading comprehension. They need a framework to help them attack the text and gain confidence in comprehending the material. Once students gain confidence and learn how to locate factual information, the teacher can phase out this technique.

There are two steps to successfully using this technique. First, the teacher writes cloze sentences. Second, the students complete the cloze activity and write summary sentences.

Framed Outline Example

Forests are filled with _____ and _____. Unlike other forests, rainforests are very _____ because they get a lot of _____.

Another type of forest is a _____ rainforest. Like rainforests, tropical rainforests are also very _____ from _____, but they are also _____. Because of this, _____ and _____ grow healthy and colorful. Temperate rainforests are _____ and _____. The fog comes from moist _____ from _____.

Summary Sentences

Tropical rainforests and temperate rainforest have many similarities and differences. Both rainforests have wet and rainy weather. Tropical rainforests are warm, which helps plant life. Temperate rainforests are foggy because of the moist air from the ocean.

Modeling Written Responses

A frequent concern of educators is that below-grade-level students write poor responses to content-area questions. This problem can be remedied if resource teachers and classroom teachers model what good answers look like. This is a technique you may want to use before asking your students to respond to the comprehension questions associated with the leveled texts in this series.

First, read the question aloud. Then display the question on the board and discuss how you would go about answering the question. Next, write the answer using a complete sentence that accurately answers the question. Repeat the procedure for several questions so that students can understand that written responses are your expectation. To take this one step further, post a variety of responses to a single question. Ask students to identify the strongest response and tell why it is strong. Have students identify the weakest answers and tell why they are weak. By doing this, you are helping students evaluate and strengthen their own written responses.

Strategies for Using the Leveled Texts (cont.)

On-Grade-Level Students

Student-Directed Learning

Because they are academically on grade level, student-directed learning activities can serve as a way to build independence and challenge this population of students toward further success. Remember to use the texts in this book as jump starts so that students will be interested in finding out more about the topics. On-grade-level students may enjoy any of the following activities:

- Write your own questions, exchange them with others, and grade each other's responses.

- Review the text and teach the topic to another group of students.

- Read other texts about the topic to further expand your knowledge.

- Create an illustrated timeline or presentation on the topic to present to the class.

- Create your own story similar to the plot in the passage read.

- Lead a discussion group around the leveled question that accompanies the text.

- Research topics from the text in depth and write a new text based on the information.

- Extend the plot of the story or write a new ending to the text.

Highlight It!

Teach students to parse out information based on the genre while they are reading. Use the chart below and a highlighter to focus students on genre-specific text features.

Genre	What do I highlight?	
fiction—historical fiction, realistic fiction, literature	characters setting theme/moral	problem solution
nonfiction—biography, autobiography, informational	leading/main idea sentence important information sequence of events	

Strategies for Using the Leveled Texts *(cont.)*

On-Grade-Level Students *(cont.)*

Detective Work

Teach students to be analytical, like detectives. Direct students' attention to text features such as titles, illustrations, and subheadings by asking students to cover the text and only look at the text features. They can use the chart below to organize analytical thinking about text features prior to reading the text.

Name of Text:		
Text Feature	Why do you think this feature was included?	What can this feature tell you about what the text might be about?
title, subtitle, and headings		
pictures, images, and captions		
diagrams and maps		

138

Strategies for Using the Leveled Texts *(cont.)*

Above-Grade-Level Students

Open-Ended Questions and Activities

Teachers need to be aware of activities that provide a ceiling that is too low for above-grade-level students. When given activities like this, these students become disengaged. These students can do more, but how much more? Offering open-ended questions and activities will provide above-grade-level students with opportunities to perform at or above their ability levels. For example, ask students to evaluate major events described in the texts, such as: "In what ways is world trade more efficient today?" or "Explain several reasons why movers should understand math." These questions require students to form opinions, think deeply about the issues, and form statements in their minds. Questions like this have lots of right answers.

The generic open-ended question stems listed here can be adapted to any topic. There is one leveled comprehension question for each text in this book. These extension question stems can be used to develop further comprehension questions for the leveled texts.

- In what ways did . . .
- How might you have done this differently . . .
- What if . . .
- What are some possible explanations for . . .
- How does this affect . . .
- Explain several reasons why . . .
- What problems does this create . . .
- Describe the ways . . .
- What is the best . . .
- What is the worst . . .
- What is the likelihood . . .
- Predict the outcome . . .
- Form a hypothesis . . .
- What are three ways to classify . . .
- Support your reason . . .
- Compare this to modern times . . .
- Make a plan for . . .
- Propose a solution to. . .
- What is an alternative to . . .

139

Strategies for Using the Leveled Texts *(cont.)*

Above-Grade-Level Students *(cont.)*

Tiered Assignments

Teachers can differentiate lessons by using tiered assignments or extension activities. These assignments are designed to have varied levels of depth, complexity, and abstractness. All students work toward one concept or outcome, but the lesson is tiered to allow for different levels of readiness and performance levels. As students work, they build on and extend their prior knowledge and understanding. Guidelines for writing tiered lessons include the following:

1. Pick the skill, concept, or generalization that needs to be learned.
2. Assess the students using classroom discussions, quizzes, tests, or journal entries.
3. Think of an on-grade level activity that teaches this skill, concept, or generalization.
4. Take another look at the activity from Step 3. Modify this activity to meet the needs of the below-grade-level and above-grade-level learners. Add complexity and depth for the above-grade-level learners. Add vocabulary support and concrete examples for the below-grade-level students.

Extension Activities Ideas

Extension activities can be used to extend the reading beyond the passages in this book. These suggested activities will help get you started. (Note: All the passages do not have extension activities.)

1. Research a rainforest in the world and then construct an informative brochure to persuade visitors to visit the rainforest.
2. Pretend you are one of Sarah's siblings. Write two journal entries about your voyage to the New World.
3. Invent your own superhero. Be sure to include his/her talent(s), ability, and claim to fame.
4. Research another body part/system that can be compared to technology
5. Find five boxes around you. Use a ruler to find the volume of each box.
6. Make your own harvest lunch menu. Be sure to list the steps you need to take to prepare the food.
7. What are some other ways people get around on water? Research and write a paragraph on the information gathered. Include an illustration.
8. Make a model of a habitat for an animal you like. Be sure to label all important parts of the habitat.
9. Make a diagram showing how pollination happens.
10. Research a rock or mineral. Use the information gathered to write an All About book.
11. Make a map of your classroom or school. Include a key and legend.
12. Research Abigail Adams. Extend her biography by writing about the rest of her life.

140

Strategies for Using the Leveled Texts *(cont.)*

English Language Learners

Effective teaching for English language learners requires effective planning. To achieve success, teachers need to understand and use a conceptual framework to help them plan lessons and units. These are the six major components to any framework:

1. **Select and Define Concepts and Language Objectives**—Before having students read one of the texts in this book, first choose a subject/concept and a language objective (listening, speaking, reading, or writing) appropriate for the grade level. The next step is to clearly define the concept to be taught. This requires knowledge of the subject matter, alignment with local and state objectives, and careful formulation of a statement that defines the concept. This concept represents the overarching idea and should be posted in a visible place in the classroom.

   By the definition of the concept, post a set of key language objectives. Based on the content and language objectives, select essential vocabulary from the text. (A list of possible words can be found on page 134.) The number of new words selected should be based on students' English language levels. Post these words on a word wall that may be arranged alphabetically or by themes.

2. **Build Background Knowledge**—Some English language learners may have a lot of knowledge in their native language, while others may have little or no knowledge. Build the background knowledge of the students using different strategies, such as the following:

   Visuals—Use posters, photographs, postcards, newspapers, magazines, drawings, and video clips of the topic you are presenting. The texts in this series include multiple images, maps, diagrams, charts, tables, and illustrations for your use.

   Realia—Bring real-life objects to the classroom. If you are teaching about reading a map, bring different types of maps, a compass, and/or a globe.

   Vocabulary and Word Wall—Introduce key vocabulary in context. Create families of words. Have students draw pictures that illustrate the words and write sentences about the words. Also be sure you have posted the words on a word wall in your classroom. (Key vocabulary from the various texts can be found on page 134.)

   Desk Dictionaries—Have students create their own desk dictionaries using index cards. On one side of each card, they should draw a picture of the word. On the opposite side, they should write the word in their own language and in English.

Strategies for Using the
Leveled Texts *(cont.)*

English Language Learners *(cont.)*

3. **Teach Concepts and Language Objectives**—Present content and language objectives clearly. Engage students by using a hook and pace the delivery of instruction, taking into consideration the students' English language levels. State the concept or concepts to be taught clearly. Use the first languages of the students whenever possible, or assign other students who speak the same languages to mentor and to work cooperatively with the English language learners.

   Lev Semenovich Vygotsky (1978), a Russian psychologist, wrote about the zone of proximal development. This theory states that good instruction must fill the gap that exists between the present knowledge of a child and the child's potential. Scaffolding instruction is an important component when planning and teaching lessons. English language learners cannot skip stages of language and content development. You must determine where the students are in the learning process and teach to the next level using several small steps to get to the desired outcome. With the leveled texts in this series and periodic assessment of students' language levels, you can support students as they climb the academic ladder.

4. **Practice Concepts and Language Objectives**—English language learners need to practice what they learn by using engaging activities. Most people retain knowledge best after applying what they learn to their own lives. This is definitely true for English language learners. Students can apply content and language knowledge by creating projects, stories, skits, poems, or artifacts that show what they have learned. Some activities should be geared to the right side of the brain, like those listed above. For students who are left-brain dominant, activities such as defining words and concepts, using graphic organizers, and explaining procedures should be developed. The following teaching strategies are effective in helping students practice both language and content:

   Simulations—Students re-create concepts in texts by becoming a part of them. They have to make decisions as if they lived in historical times. For example, students can pretend that they are Sarah, an immigrant traveling to America. They have to describe and act out the conditions of her voyage to the New World. Or, students can act out a fictional passage by pretending they are one of the superheroes described. They can reenact the passage, while extending their understanding of the superheroes' abilities and claims to fame.

   Literature response—Read a text from this book. Have students choose two people described or introduced in the text. Ask students to write conversations the people might have. Or you can have students write journal entries about events in the daily lives of the important people. Literature responses can also include student opinions, reactions, and questions about texts.

Strategies for Using the Leveled Texts *(cont.)*

English Language Learners *(cont.)*

4. Practice Concepts and Language Objectives *(cont.)*

Have a short debate—Make a controversial statement such as, "We can live without rules." After reading a text in this book, have students think about the question and take a position. As students present their ideas, one student can act as a moderator.

Interview—Students may interview a member of their family or a neighbor in order to obtain information regarding a topic from the texts in this book. For example: How is your life similar to the lives of African Americans in the 1930s?

5. Evaluation and Alternative Assessments—Evaluation should be used to inform instruction. Students must have opportunities to show their understandings of concepts in different ways and not only through standard assessments. Use both formative and summative assessments to ensure that you are effectively meeting your content and language objectives. Formative assessment is used to plan effective lessons for particular groups of students. Summative assessment is used to find out how much the students have learned. Other authentic assessments that show day-to-day progress are: text retelling, teacher rating scales, student self-evaluations, cloze statements, holistic scoring of writing samples, performance assessments, and portfolios. Periodically assessing student learning will help you ensure that students continue to receive the correct levels of texts.

6. Home/School Connection—The home/school connection is an important component in the learning process for English language learners. Parents are the first teachers, and they establish expectations for their children. These expectations help shape the behavior of their children. By asking parents to be active participants in the education of their children, students get double doses of support and encouragement. As a result, families become partners in the education of their children and chances for success in your classroom increase.

You can send home copies of the texts in this series for parents to read with their children. You can even send multiple levels to meet the needs of your second-language parents as well as your students. In this way, you are sharing what you are covering in the classroom with your whole second language community.

Resources

Contents of Digital Resource CD

PDF Files

The full-color PDFs provided are each six pages long and contain all three levels of a reading passage. For example, *What Are Rainforests?* (pages 11–16) is the *rainforests.pdf* file.

Text Files

The Microsoft Word® documents include the text for all three levels of each reading passage. For example, *What Are Rainforests?* (pages 11–16) is the *rainforests.docx* file.

Text Title	Text File	PDF
What Are Rainforests?	rainforests.docx	rainforests.pdf
Dr. Martin Luther King Jr.	mlkjr.docx	mlkjr.pdf
Sarah's Journal	journal.docx	journal.pdf
Your Guide to Superheroes	superheroes.docx	superheroes.pdf
The World's Fastest Computer	computer.docx	computer.pdf
Lots of Boxes	boxes.docx	boxes.pdf
Planning a Harvest Lunch	harvestlunch.docx	harvestlunch.pdf
Getting Around on the Water	onthewater.docx	onthewater.pdf
Markets in India	marketsindia.docx	marketsindia.pdf
City Gardens	citygardens.docx	citygardens.pdf
Wonderful Water	water.docx	water.pdf
What Makes a Habitat?	habitat.docx	habitat.pdf
Pollination	pollination.docx	pollination.pdf
Rocks and Minerals	rocksminerals.docx	rocksminerals.pdf
Solids	solids.docx	solids.pdf
Rules to Live By	rules.docx	rules.pdf
Trade Today	trade.docx	trade.pdf
Lead the Way!	lead.docx	lead.pdf
Using Maps	maps.docx	maps.pdf
Young Abigail Adams	abigailadams.docx	abigailadams.pdf

Word Documents of Texts

- Change leveling further for individual students.
- Separate text and images for students who need additional help decoding the text.
- Resize the text for visually impaired students.

Digital Resource CD

Full-Color PDFs of Texts

- Project texts for whole-class review.
- Post on your website and read texts online.
- Email texts to parents or students at home.